To Dream
A Little . . .

With Best Wishes,

R. Roberts

To Dream A Little . . .

R.J. Roberts

To order additional copies of this book, contact:
Xlibris Corporation
0-800-644-6988
www.xlibrispublishing.co.uk
Orders@xlibrispublishing.co.uk
301236

Contents

To my Parents and Brother
With Love

Special Thanks to my father who nagged and persevered with me
in publishing this little book and also to Mum for coming up with
a title. This is for you both.

Introduction

This poetry collection was written during the transition of my childhood to adulthood years. They were based on my memories of scenes that I have witnessed and events that were significant to me. There are also personal poems close to my heart, which were expressed or conveyed with emotions or feelings that a reader may relate to.

So I am delighted to share my first poetry collection with all readers out there and hope this would inspire to take their dream further and see it in reality.

Happy reading!

Dreams

Dreams forever in minds,
not long-lost and forgotten;
The soul in your wishful eyes,
dreams in your heart,
the moon beckons the corner of your eye,
pierces right through your soul;
Dream spirit 'words' through your eyes;
forever entwined,
a promise not far off
is in your Destiny.

My Soul—A Desert

My soul was empty,
like a vast, arid, barren place,
a desert, baked under the glaring sun,
longing for its stream of water.
My mind began to wander,
jagged thoughts tumbled around
splintered emotions cut hard,
like a spring breaking through
the icy hold of winter.
To feed my soul,
a quest for happiness seemed oblivious
walked from Bethlehem to Jerusalem,
my feet became sore,
with blisters that hurt.
Won't you carry me?

For my heart is laden with heaviness,
the lambent beauty of the soul
beholds me,
seeing other souls in the throes
of Machiavelli moods,
for now, I know I have been carried,
my soul; no longer a desert
my soul has found
the corner of paradise.

Old Folks

I stood staring through the window,
seeing old people's faces filling the space,
wrinkle after wrinkle, telling the years of hardship;
The irises of their eyes held the wisest nature of their lives;
Seeing the smiles on their faces and understanding the meaning of happiness.
Their rough hands with cragged edges, used to shape and mould their future ahead.
Their ungainly figures walked along the same road.
I pressed my face harder on the window,
the mist of breath covered it.
Old, weary faces vanished,
left me staring through the window.

Who Am I?

Born in this world,
born to be part of this wild creation,
the vast blue dome,
trees weeping in the cruel wind,
tears of leaves falling to the ground,
sorrowful flowers drooping their heads,
the sea raging in turmoil as the waves
clash against each other,
the force of nature binding together as one part of life.

Who am I? What is life?
Seeing the wonderful things,
the comet of brightness
zooming past my heart,
my life as the sun revolving round and round,
the planets of the universe engulfing in a cloak of galaxies of stars,
The mysterious darkness descends above my head.
Life has a purpose, hasn't it?
What is the secret of my existence?
Existence starts from a small seed to become a big, vast universe,
Existence is my life;
From uncreation to creation.
What seeks beyond my life?
How far is it beyond there?
Am I here of my own free will?
Or are we just a "lie"?

The sun gleaming with pretence,
the rain showering with sadness,
the winter snowing with bitterness,
the summer sky with laziness,
the spring tuning the raw beauty,
the end of my fingertips beckons the preciousness
of life,
wishful dreams, high hopes,
what could be truer than life?

The force of nature in my body,
holding me tightly, not letting me go,
holding my precious life;
not driving it away,
Who is ruling my mind?
Who is ruling my heart?
Is my mind ruling my heart?
Is my heart ruling my mind?
Except, who controls my existence,
My life, my being?

An Ordinary Day

Lying in the sun-weathered sand,
feeling the wind on my body,
seeing the untouchable white clouds that
move with subtle timelessness.
The spherical arch above me,
the sweeping azure blue sky stretches infinitely.
Enveloped in primordial earth-like globe,
watching everyday, as life passes by me motionlessly.
Looking ahead, the majestic Ouranas looks further and further.
My fingers can only reach so far,
but my mind can travel further.
The imagination fulfils the expectations
of what lies beyond the expanse of the great Ouranas,
on an ordinary day.

- Ouranas—This is a Greek term defining the 'sky' or 'heaven'

Human Nature

The loving gestures that come from
the heart or the mind, or the invisible soul,
the presence of thoughts.
Wisdom harbours the
consciousness of the mind,
conscience of the heart,
our actions betray our weaknesses,
Is understanding and compassion borne
within us or did human nature rob us of the altruistic virtues?
Are we not bounded to the rules of virtues that guide us?
Only the vain and arrogant that vex us like heavy dark passing clouds.
They seek no reasons to malign the good-natured ones.
Their conscience is not carved on their hearts, nor their desire compel the
    consciousness of the mind.
Blinded by false pretences, they only see the mirage of beauty,
Enamoured ones profit the grace of appreciation;
The unwanted, unappreciated souls strive to fill the void
in their hearts waiting for.
A simple loving act or gesture that can make 'you' a whole person.

The Peaceman's Journey

I no longer *see,*
I no longer *hear,*
I no longer *speak.*
Where did my thoughts go?
To some unknown place,
the abyss of the mind,
where the sun no longer shines,
only the coolness rising upwards,
feeling the aching sadness,
where soul trod alone.
My *voice* goes unheard,
silence languishes,
my eyes, no *sight,*
for there is no light,
only frozen visions trapped.
Can I hear you?

Mirthless, for there is no *sound*,
only stillness in cold moments.
The solidarity of the *mind*
fills with light,
shadows ebb away,
grasping my soul,
the soul found its place.
A place of sound, sight, smell, and sense.
My journey was not alone.

The Millennium Future?

The rich, earthly soil
Toiling beneath our unmajestic feet;
Merging with human nature,
Born of the flesh,
Like a seedling in thirsty ground.

War and terror ravaged and trampled
On the souls in dust.
Words perished before us,
Nature defied nature.

The flesh succumbed in yawning darkness,
Where jackals roamed and devoured.
Scattered us among nations,
With silent fear,
That wept before terror.
Death reaped the rich and poor,
Plunged them into deep mire.

Will flowers flourish where the sweet nectar flows freely?
Will the river swell abundantly where their pastures yield its fruits?
Will the animals dwell in place which the forest bestows upon them?

How death scorns us!

Will the blind people see raptures and delights?
Will the dumb people shout in triumph?
Will the deaf people hear words of wisdom?
Will immobile people walk the vast dominions?

How empty and vain are their words
Which fall like ashes!
Your days are like conspicuous shadows,
where no earthly joy shall fill them.

What is the dream?

Do you remember Martin Luther King who fought for the Promised
Land for black people?
Do you remember Nelson Mandela who gave Freedom to South Africa?
Do you remember Helen Keller who spoke from strength to strength for
disabled people?
Do you remember Thomas Edison who shone light to the world,
dispersing darkness?
Can we rise up with our noble dreams from the dust of ashes?

Do you remember their dreams?

What can subdue us?

Greed, lies, envy;
You, men, women that pride themselves,
Are prey within yourselves.
Fallen away in a breath of oppression
Where deceit and power ransom our souls.

Death shall not prevail over us.

The rich, earthly soil
Toiling beneath our unmajestic feet;
All nations, our dominion,
Like a seedling in thirsty ground,
It shall prosper in glory.

Nottingham

Nottingham is the past
and the future;
like dreams that lie
forgotten,
it stays in our souls
through and through,
where the Nottinghamshire lands
tells of tales,
through Sherwood Forest
where Robin Hood roamed.
He serves as a reminder
of the past.
Upon the cobbled roads stood
the fortress of Nottingham Castle,
a legacy for its people,
down along the road,
where weary travellers
stop by Old Salutation Inn
for a meal and a rest.
In the Market Square,
filled with carriages of horses
going slowly by,
flower girls filling the scents in the air,
up along the road,
the Nag's Head serves its last ale
to a convict.

Rows of graves in the known cemetery, entomb
the old, the young and soldiers who lived to hear and see
the tales of Nottingham.
Oh, Renowned beloved city
on a threshold of a
New Millennium,
A hoped-for time of happiness
for all who dwell in thee!
Nottingham is our past
and the future.

Ceylon

Part I

The pearl island floats quietly on a bed of Ocean, laced with historical
    tales.
The golden palm fringed beaches carry their salty breath across.
The elephants roamed in the vicinity of "Elephant Pass",
the golden Buddha mediates in the land of Pollanaruwa.
The pleasure Garden of Demon*sheltered in Nuwara Eliya.
The scent of tea leaves enshrouded in the heart of Kandy.
The taste of Golden B.O.P *filled our tongues.
Great Kaduganawa, Balane, and Haputale mountains bowed down before
    us, near Opiah Pass haven to the Bambarandkanda Falls,
Veiled in mists;
The wild hills bestow orchids and anthuriums in the Garden of
    Peradeniya.
Acres and acres of exotic delights haunt us.
As dusk falls, smeared in palest pink watercolour, the heat of the sun
    embraces us,
The stars jewelled like falling embers.
The sounds of our mother tongue
"Vanakkam", "Ayebowan"
Greets us welcome.

Part II

> Poverty edged to the tips of the pearl island,
> where the last trickle of water seeps into the barren land,
> where the vine of the branches withered away,
> no longer bearing its fruits,
> where justice pales into insignificance.
> Distended bellies starved of its comfort,
> rocky roads drove for miles in endless mire.
> The jaded pearl torn asunder,
> its veil cast doubts and fears.
> As the sun moves East,
> leaving darkness all around,
> the waning moon drowns all its sorrows.
> The days are not over and yet still to come.

Notes

1. The pleasure Garden of Demon—King of Lanka, Ravana of Ramayana Epic
2. B.O.P—Broken Orange Pekoe

Sweet Dear Old Carolina

Sweet North Carolina,
her golden hair fanned like golden plain rocks.
Her cool blue liquid forming little tearful streams.
her cheeks blushed at the sight of the scornful sun.
Her arms and legs bronzed with rich brown colour of the deserts.
Her voice filled with the soulful blue melodies.
A gust of wind grazed her cheeks and catches her breath.
Her big beating heart pulsates, sweet, soft, and flowing
inner land rises gracefully, carved deep with harsh, rough cragged peripheral
    edges that jagged along the lengths.
Her warmth invites all.
The universe with might looked upon the vast dominion.
That is the dear old Carolina.

Africa

The safari coolness of the moon hung
as a watch light over the dangerous territory;
The brazen land trembles before its guard,
where the ivory elephants walked with a gentle sway,
The tiger eye revelled beneath the forest glade Leaves,
preying for its claim,
a honey-coloured deer trekked alluringly,
its tiger stripes caged the elusive prize.
"Iningizimu Africa, Izwe lethu, Izwe lobabamkhulu"*
The ancestors nimble and barefooted,
their dark chocolate eyes rolled
down to their deep, satiny bellies.
The scent of power unmistakeably noticed.
Zebras patrolled anxiously like watchmen,
the tall summer-tanned giraffes
promenading like faithful old servants of the land.
Under the safari moon, the stillness of the night;
sitting on the treacherous rocks,
the observant chameleon eye watched.

*Translates as "South Africa, our country, country of our
forefathers"—Zulu*

Cova Da Iria

Soft olive fields freshly laid out;
basking under the soft fiery globe,
beating the brows of the hills,
smooth ridges slope downwards,
blowing wind gathers up the swirling dust,
parched dry virgin soil gently roasted,
quiet stillness sculpted an ever-beautiful landscape,
a timeless Cova Da Iria sits among the hills and fields;
unnoticed by people who creep in every day.

Love

Love has no bounds.
Love is like a sea, washed with waves of passion.
Love is like sand that trickles through your fingers.
Love is like the clouds of your heart.
Love is like a sun that shines radiantly.
Love is the queen of dreams.
Love is love.
Love is pure, divine, powerful, and beautiful.
Love is like a raindrop that never disappears.
Love that comes from the unspoken mouth to say "I Love You".

Unrequited Love

Through clouds and sunshine,
time passing never disappears,
memories locked away in sweet yonder heart;
at the dawn and at the end of a day,
my unfailing hope never goes away.
Sweet memories glimpsed in one's heart;
those dreamy blue eyes of skies
rain bowed in kindness,
stained forever like golden dust,
falling from the dark velvety sky,
mistress of the moon, the land, and the sea
whispered the past of the good times
a sorrowful goodbye;
through clouds and sunshine,
shall I never part from you.

Haunted Memories

Dreams stained in mind,
Memories haunted every crevices of me;
Thorns around me, bitingly,
Consumed sadness over my broken body,
Treacherous, weeping thoughts
Drowning in a sea of agony,
No turning back the years,
Dead, lost, and forgotten,
Doomed, nonetheless, reawakened,
Nothing in return
Memories—never cease.

Imagination

Lie back; let your mind wander,
Set yourself in an idyllic place,
Imagine being in an Elysian field of contented beauty,
Like a quaint picture hanging on your wall.

Let the space fill your mind,
Darkness covers your entire mind,
Bring yourself the colours of imagination,
Swallow yourself in a vortex of kaleidoscope,
Pass yourself through time and space.

Picture yourself as queen of the meadow,
Let sweet peas, honeysuckles, and violets
Tickle your mind in riot.
Lie back; let the warmth caress you,
Let your mind travel, filling the spaces.

See the calico sky above you,
Sense yourself at the liberty of your lair,
Hear the murmur of the streams,
Feel your feet sink beneath the golden sand,
Time eclipsed in your mind.

Tell me, what do you see?
Lamenting sound of the waves
Brought you back in the quake of darkness.

Imagination—powerful in the eye of your mind.

Deafness

As I opened my eyes,
I see myriad of colours,
that speak the language of beauty and mystery;
the droning noise goes on and on,
like a worm festering in its hole,
that makes no cruel sound.

When morning comes,
the sweet smell of
sun-drenched flowers,
brimming with perfection,
the sounds disassemble
like old ruin of cities.

Where a thousand voices
gleamed with its saturnine smiles,
a humming, burgeoning noise
grates within its organ.

My eyes of impregnable silence,
to hear a voice,
simply divine,
Yes, from me to you
my eyes becomes my ears.

Drink Me

Drink Me . . . for I look so ripe!
Orange, lushly and in flesh,
Drink me . . . the sun is hot,
Orange, red, and yellow rays,
So succulent and so sweet,
Makes your thirsty taste buds feverish,
Your only drink, your dream,
The juicy segments veined with 'secrets',
Come and taste me . . . drink me . . .
Your parched throat, dying for desire
Taste the glory of the bittersweet juices!
Oh! What a revelation!

Temper

Temper! Temper!
Rotting inside me like madness;
Feel unwanted by people who are filled with gladness;
Deadly thoughts flock around like ravens;
Soothing comforts beckon me to crave.
Threat of darts trapped in my hands;
Wanting to disappear from the land;
Temper! Temper!

The Sky

The cloudless sky above me,
clear as crystal,
the sun shone like a golden ball,
drinking in those vibrant colours,
fiery red, yellow, and orange streaks,
like an Indian Summer in the forest
among the wild hills and heathers,
gentle breeze blew through with a kiss from the past;
the colourful streaks washed away,
a calming darkness ebbed over the sky.
A summer storm crashed through,
streams of Nile wept on top of me,
so cool and yet so warm as the summer,
sweet inspiration tantalized through me.
The defiant sun rose up with a cloak of golden streaks;
the beautiful cloudless azure sky
looked so sound, so sound above me.

Goodbye

When time comes,
You are never far from home,
Yesterday is gone,
Please stay with me, just for today,
The sunset fades away,
The moon forever hung silently.
Desolate cries in ears,
Sweet, soft murmurs never left the mind.
Hold me tightly,
Remembering you, remember me always,
Please stay with me, just for today,
Until then
I kissed you goodbye.

Venus

Soft, icy globe,
Clipped, crisp, snow-dusted wings,
Cool, stark-white hands clasped my robe,
Surrounded by pale queens and kings.

Venus—cold, blue-tight lipped
Wintry breath bit my cheeks.
Hot molten liquid inside me ripped,
Cold, blue-satin eyes that seeks.

Warm, smouldering breath enveloped me,
Thy beauty has faded,
None for all to see,
Thy silver wings became jaded.

If dreams fail, has no place,
Consumed desire dies,
And I; broken, fallen grace;
Vestige of emotions undisturbed lies.

Flames vanquished forever.

Ice-time

Skating on thin ice,
Agile as a butterfly,
Weaving and gliding gently,
Watching the smooth, sleek
Spinning circles formed on ice;
Like a passing sable cloud,
A rush of adrenaline pounds,
Wielding the hockey stick,
A smooth instrument of a dangerous edge,
Moving forward in sharp cutting gestures,
Born out of ice,
Riding high and aiming ambitiously,
Ruthlessly like a storm brewing up silently,
Holding in a calculated precision
To claim the goal again.

Blue Eyes

Blue ethereal eyes piercing
in the midst of my mind;
Long strands curling around my slender neck;
Feeling every breath tingling down my spine;
Soft, yielding presence wraps around my hands and feet,
cool blue electric atmosphere netting around my passive body.
Untouched, detached, yet charged alive with feelings,
whispers reverberate in my ears;
Coming out of a dream-like reverie,
cold, sleepless, impassive blue eyes stares through me;
And steals my soul.

Time Travel

Time is my enemy!
Time is my friend?
2010
            2009
                        2008 keep clocking
Hear the tick-tock sounds mocking,
What can I do, my friend?
                        1860
            1820
1800
Laid in a forgotten land,
Where minutes, seconds, and hours trickled
Ubiquitously like sand.
Take a leap back,
A hundred years of mystique surrounded,
Time of appreciation is founded.
Time travelling is a grain
Of a dream.

The October Cat

A black alley creature walked lightly
under the silvery October moon.
Two small fangs spangled like sharp-blade knives.
Tiptoeing on little claws that dug hard on the
stony pavement.
Green eyes quivered against the dark pitch night.
Small cackle rustled through the silver lime trees.
A small hump on the back with black sinful silky fur rippling.
An old woman walked with her black handbag clutched tightly.
Eyes sagged beneath the thick spidery lashes.
Her legs with trace of blue veins like blue stilton cheese.
A shrilling noise shook the sound of the air.
A black creature jumped out and ran like a thief in the dark.
Beware of the black witch's October cat.

Twin Towers

I stand tall with pride, might, and liberty
through twenty-seven years of changes.
At the dawn of day, the sleepy sun rises up
to greet me with warmth;
As evening draws, the sunset glistens in
my reflection like a strong armour
withstood all the elements.
My dream earned a place in a mirage of postcards
and people's memories.
Next to my twin, we stood united
Today, Tomorrow, Next Year
has ended.
Sunbursts preyed upon us,
hundreds and hundreds of souls aflame,
I see him imploded with dignity and disintegrate
in my own reflections.
My dream shattered like fallen dusts,
obliterated in minutes.
Today, Tomorrow, Next Year,
I will rise up in endurance to fulfil my dream once again!

The Master

The monitor flickers
staring down at me,
silently with no compunctions.
I would stare back,
mindlessly at the courier new jargon,
sitting boldly in their places.
The master has spoken its language,
clocking at 400 MHz ahead of me.
RAM knows me, taking 64 MB of memory lane trip into account,
With cutting efficiency.
As I reached the final point,
the master performs one final act,
it initiates the command,
after brief micro-seconds,
The master's friend ALU helps to execute with sophistication.
The ultimate goal has been sought.

A Nonsensical Poem

The darkness of the night
advances slowly through the streets,
searching and seeking the silver moon.
The dark and pale roses are glistening
in the twilight.
A man with a grey face is touching the fog of the past.

Free Spirit

Thundering hooves gallop across the plains,
dust swirling like dancing storms,
his long dark mane flies effortlessly in the wind,
his glossy, sheer coat belies the straining,
honed muscles, exerting the power and force
that propels them forward,
like a soaring bird in the sky.
His sixth sense guides him,
no rules, no duties, and no constraints
bounds him to his master.
Miles stretched before him,
the white cumulus clouds
so white like mountains,
hard to reach them, but can see them.
Sounds of hooves marched freely,
as his heart beats beneath him,
his wise soulful eyes can see the inner part
of you, it knows what it wants.
No direction to hold him back,
Unseparated by nature but by man,
bridled with strength and fervour,
pounding in the sun, heading towards the
Freedom's gate.

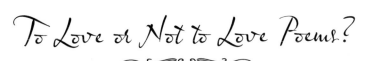

To Love or Not to Love Poems?

A poem is a secret message,
a poem is a mouth that opens,
to reveal love, grief, nature, sin, and hope
in utter anguish of breath.
A poem divided in black and white with a stem of justice.
A poem must be loved as well as with other people.
A poem must be read in the light,
not left in the darkness.

Dedicated to a Friend

Red, orange, brown crinkly leaves
Fallen liked burned fragments,
Harsh, bitter breath beating around my face;
Fury in the sky, toil and snares in my heart;
Gaping wounds branches; stripped and bared for all to see.
Summer is reborn; wild cherry trees
Blossomed, ripe, red, and luscious.
Softly, dust motes fall around me;
Sun kisses on my cheeks gently,
He who lives again!

The Sunbird

(Dedicated to a Friend)

Sweet May, happy May?
Perfect, tumbling, gleaming
clouds circling like multitude of orbs;
Radiant light burst forth, a red rose
majestically opening its petals.
His hair, burnt russet leaves falls,
flames glowing within his heart.
The blue sky, luminous with love and warmth;
pale light fades, the capricious wind dies,
sounds dissolves into obscurity;
The sunbird flapping against Time,
ventured far beyond the tumbling,
gleaming *and* perfect clouds.

The Humble Pilgrim

An old church stood along Brooklyn Road,
Built of bricks and mortar,
Saturated with a hundred years of faith,
Homage paid by fellow pilgrims.

A humble presence stirs your heart,
A palpable sense permeates through your body,
A draught of coolness wraps around your legs,
The sacred road begins your journey.

Rows of pews of mahogany gleamed,
Generation by generation sat before the crowning altar,
On the third row sat a humble pilgrim,
Equally known as "Mr Davison".

Songs of old revives the ageing atmosphere,
His wondrous wise nature beguiles us all,
Leading a very simple dedicated life,
Always close at God's hand.

His steadfast faith, firm as a rock,
Waxen candles flicker timelessly,
Never fading nor dimming,
A light prevails over darkness.

With his walking stick in one hand,
Cloaked in a heavy tweed coat, his green hat donned,
Led by the Spirit,
The sacred road has come to an end.

Wild Bill

Tall, wiry, lean Wild Bill,
Who had his fill,
Of women and wine,
He liked to dine.

Leaving town for gold,
None he could hold,
Armed in six-shooter,
Slaying outlaws and looters.

Willow trees and plains,
Where outlaws have lain,
Two eights and aces,
McCall strides in paces.

Shot in the head,
Wild Bill was dead,
His days were numbered,
Ghostly Deadwood was rumbled.

His life forever known,
The legacy is sown,
He lies in peace,
His legend never ceased.

Line 4—Wild Bill often frequented in Long Saloon Branch, where his deadly reputation was known

Line 7—He was famous for his six-shooter.

Line 10—He also had several well-known friends such as Jesse James and possibly John. W. Hardin

Line 11—A pair of eights and aces was left in his hand when he was shot. It became known as 'Dead Man's Hand'

Line 12—Jack McCall was responsible for Wild Bill's death. It is not known what Jack McCall's motive was.

Line 15—Wild Bill had a premonition that may have foreseen his death. So he knew his days were numbered.

Line 16—Wild Bill has served Abilene as Marshall. He came to Deadwood, possibly because he was offered a job there.

Line 17—Wild Bill is buried in South Dakota. His death was re-enacted every year, in Deadwood, USA.

An Assurance

God chose an unexpected,
Ordinary place to appear
And when I least expected.
I recognised Him and His presence
In the ordinariness of my life.
Everything was in short supply,
He was the food of strength,
friendship, and hope for me.
A miracle, one to lift me up,
To give me strength and hope
To carry on and to feel fine.
I "regained" myself and all is well
again.

Courage

As I walked along the twisted forked paths
Leading to nowhere,
Blanketed in tempestuous flame-red leaves
Obscuring the true path.
Cruel, deformed fingers arched over their
Stripped, bare trunks, reaching out insidiously.
My mind lost at the ocean,
Icy blue deceptive waves swirled in beguiling calmness
Against each other,
Silently the malicious undercurrents breaches the stream
Of consciousness.
Lost in the middle of an ocean with no oars of guidance,
Falling into a deep bottomless void.
My feet clutching the slippery, silky slopes
As I climb the strength of the mountain,
Slipping step by step before I can catch myself.
But who can catch me?
What must I do to fight and survive against the odds?
How can I learn to move the might of a mountain before me?
The winds of willpower gravitates myself forward,
"Seek and you shall find it"
I find myself climb the strength of the mountain once more.

Child of My Heart

(Jessica)

My child of my heart,
Whose head asleep upon my breast,
Enrobed in its finest silk and cloth,
Adorned with coppery hair,
Will the Rapunzelian mane
Fall sleekly down her back?
Or will the rolling curls entwine
Around my fingers?
When the April showers,
The westerly wind blows,
The birth of the goddess sun descends,
While her pretty fingers clasped my own,
A kiss upon her rosy hues,
Her beauty transcends,
Confounds the sweet whispers to rest.

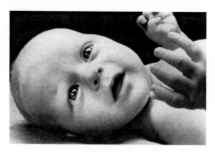

My Brother

We shared our childhood dreams and secrets,
shared our tears, fun, laughter, and joy
together as the years passed us by.
A vivid memory of playing together,
rode our bicycles, picking you up in times of trouble,
and telling each other stories.
You stood by me in the hour of need,
your astuteness shaped my thoughts with modern,
creative and inspiring touches—never judging me.
Full of charm and all knowing,
your smile illuminates me, lifting my thoughts upwards,
your strength becomes my strength.
My best friend, thank you for being there always.

Dream Child

Under the cool May sky,
the blessings of spring time.
A young woman whose innocence and beauty transcends,
bestowed with gifts and wisdom, she descends.
Long soft ebony hair gently swaying in the wind of May almost too soft
to catch it.
A golden sun, majestically but not too soon,
nor hiding behind the waxen moon.
A true dream child holds Amma's and Iya's hearts;
Such a worthy child, nor silver and gold can possess.
A dream child: my friend: my mother.

Dream Bird

Dreams are like cobwebs;
Fragile yet full of hope.
Beautiful, iridescent colours splashed on those
pretty fragile wings.
Those wings that carry us through the seasons,
we weathered the storms together in difficult times.
Rays of sunlight lifted us up from our strife.
The dream bird we see through night and day flitters
amongst the cobwebs of dreams; the little wisdom of truths written on a
wind of clouds,
memories close to our hearts.
As the sun goes down, those wings that once again swept the shadows away.
Morning comes again, behind the gleaming star, the majestic clouds,
on a single branch, we know we will see you again . . .

The Sun King

He rises up in crowning glory,
As a new chapter of a dawn telling a story.
We wake up to his greeting,
Me, us, and him are always meeting;
Everyday of the hour, minutes, seconds,
Yet even faraway, his light beckons.
His warmth envelopes me, us: a cherished moment in delight.
His radiance transforms our fears, anxieties, and sufferings into hope and
    happiness in one revealing sight.
Like seasons that come and go, always there in our shadows; never fades.
When your light reaches us and touches us, in your global presence, your
    light always stays.

Lightning Source UK Ltd.
Milton Keynes UK
30 March 2011

170110UK00002B/33/P